Table of Contents

Title:

INTRODUCTION

Copyright

CHAPTER ONE

UNDERSTANDING MICROSOFT COPILOT AI AND OPTIMIZING PRODUCTIVITY WITH ITS TOOLS

- Getting started with Microsoft Copilot AI
- The AI Revolution and Its Impact
- Copilot AI's Place in Microsoft's AI Ecosystem
- Key Features and Capabilities
- Microsoft 365: Elevating Collaboration and Productivity
- Azure AI: Harnessing the Power of Cloud AI
- Designer: Bringing Ideas to Life with AI-Powered Design
- Teams: Streamlining Communication and Teamwork
- Power Platform: Automating Processes and Workflows

CHAPTER TWO

IDENTIFYING NICHE MARKETS AND CRAFTING AI SOLUTIONS

- Understanding Niche Markets and Their Potential
- Conducting Market Research and Analysis
- Ideating and Developing AI-Powered Solutions
- Validating and Testing Your AI Solution
- Pivoting and Refining Your Approach

CHAPTER THREE

BUILDING A SUSTAINABLE ONLINE BUSINESS

- Developing a Solid Business Plan
- Securing Funding and Investments
- Scaling and Growing Your Online Business

Managing Resources and Finances
Building a Strong Brand and Online Presence

CHAPTER FOUR

MARKETING STRATEGIES FOR AI PRODUCTS AND SERVICES
Understanding the AI Market Landscape
Crafting Compelling Marketing Campaigns
Leveraging Social Media and Influencer Marketing
Content Marketing and Thought Leadership
Measuring and Optimizing Your Marketing Efforts

CHAPTER FIVE

UNDERSTANDING COPILOT AI'S CAPABILITIES
Natural Language Processing and Conversational AI
Text Generation and Content Creation
Data Analysis and Visualization
Task Automation and Process Optimization
AI-Powered Coding and Development

CHAPTER SIX

CONTENT CREATION AND COPILOT AI
Writing Engaging Blog Posts and Articles
Crafting Compelling Sales Copy
Developing Instructional and Training Materials
Generating Social Media Content
AI-Assisted Copywriting and Editing

CHAPTER SEVEN

DATA ANALYSIS WITH COPILOT AI
Extracting Insights from Complex Datasets
Building Interactive Data Visualizations
Forecasting and Predictive Modeling

Automating Routine Data Tasks
   Integrating AI with Business Intelligence Tools
CHAPTER EIGHT
  PROCESS AUTOMATION AND WORKFLOWS
     Streamlining Administrative and Office Tasks
     Automating Customer Service and Support
     Optimizing Project Management Processes
     Integrating AI into Existing Workflows
     Building Custom AI-Powered Solutions
CHAPTER NINE
  AI-POWERED CODING AND DEVELOPMENT
     Code Generation and Assistance
     AI-Driven Software Testing and Debugging
     Rapid Prototyping and Iterative Development
     Integrating AI into Existing Applications
     Exploring Emerging AI Development Frameworks
     Upcoming Features and Enhancements
     Expanding AI Capabilities
     Predictions for AI in Business Tools
     Microsoft's Vision for AI Integration
CONCLUSION

Title:
How To Make Money With Microsoft Copilot

The Complete Guide To Mastering Microsoft AI To Enhance Productivity, Streamline Workflows And Unlock Passive Income

By: Andrew G. Willard

INTRODUCTION

A ground-breaking technology has arisen to completely rethink productivity in today's fast-paced society, where work demands frequently override our intrinsic need for fulfilment and purpose. With the ability to utilize next-generation artificial intelligence and recover the essence of our work, Microsoft 365 Copilot is set to become the ultimate catalyst for unleashing our creative potential. Humans are fundamentally imaginative, creative, and inventive creatures. We all want to work on projects that fulfil our greatest dreams, whether it's penning a gripping book, discovering ground-breaking new information, creating thriving communities, or giving caring care. But the terrible truth is that we spend a lot of our time doing tedious, uninteresting things, which saps our creativity, energy, and time—the very things we need to pursue our passions.

But what if there was a way to break free from this cycle of monotony? What if we could seamlessly integrate cutting-edge technology into our workflows, allowing us to focus on the soul of our work while AI handles the tedious tasks?

This is precisely what Microsoft 365 Copilot promises to deliver.

Copilot is a conversational AI assistant that allows users to perform various tasks through natural language inputs. It can retrieve specific information, generate textual content like emails and summaries, create images based on text descriptions, and even write code in popular programming languages such as JavaScript, C, and Python. Users simply need to provide prompts in plain language, and Copilot will interpret and execute the requested actions, presenting the results in a chat-like interface. By harnessing the power of large language models (LLMs) and seamlessly integrating with the Microsoft Graph and Microsoft 365 applications, Copilot transforms our words into the most powerful productivity tool on the planet. With this groundbreaking technology, we can transcend the limitations of traditional computing and embrace a new era of human-machine collaboration.

How To Make Money With Microsoft Copilot: The Complete Guide To Mastering Microsoft AI To Enhance Productivity, Streamline Workflows And Unlock Passive Income examines the vast potential of Microsoft 365 Copilot, unveils its transformative capabilities and provides actionable strategies to harness its power. Whether you're an entrepreneur seeking to streamline operations, a professional striving for greater efficiency, or an individual passionate about personal growth, this book will equip you with the knowledge and tools to leverage Copilot and unlock a world of opportunities. Prepare to kick-start the journey that will redefine your relationship with work, ignite your creativity, and ultimately, empower you to achieve your dreams and aspirations like never before.

COPYRIGHT

All rights reserved. No part of this book may be reproduced or transmitted in any form or by any means, electronic or mechanical, including photocopying, recording, or by any information storage and retrieval system, without permission in writing from the publisher. except in the case of brief quotations embodied in critical reviews and certain other non-commercial uses permitted by copyright law.

Copyright © 2024 by Andrew G. Willard

CHAPTER ONE

UNDERSTANDING MICROSOFT COPILOT AI AND OPTIMIZING PRODUCTIVITY WITH ITS TOOLS

Getting Started With Microsoft Copilot Ai

Artificial intelligence (AI) is transforming the way we live, work, and conduct business in the modern era. Microsoft Copilot AI stands at the forefront of this technological revolution, offering a suite of powerful tools designed to streamline processes, enhance productivity, and unlock new opportunities for individuals and organizations alike. Microsoft Copilot is a suite of AI-powered tools integrated into various Microsoft products to enhance productivity and streamline workflows. Leveraging advanced artificial intelligence and machine learning algorithms, Microsoft Copilot assists users by automating repetitive tasks, providing intelligent suggestions, and facilitating more efficient collaboration. Microsoft Copilot AI is an advanced

AI system that leverages natural language processing and machine learning algorithms to understand and respond to human inputs intelligently. Microsoft Copilot AI brings the discovery of opportunities to revolutionize your approach to work, business, and personal endeavors.

Microsoft 365 Copilot represents a paradigm shift in how we work with productivity software. It introduces an entirely new way of interacting with applications and performing tasks. Copilot operates in two distinct modes:

1. Integration with Familiar Apps: Copilot is seamlessly embedded within the core Microsoft 365 applications that users rely on daily, such as Word, Excel, PowerPoint, Outlook, and Teams. This integration allows users to leverage Copilot's capabilities directly within the applications they're already accustomed to, enhancing their existing workflows.

2. Business Chat: Microsoft has unveiled an innovative new experience called Business Chat. This feature harnesses the power of large language models (LLMs), Microsoft 365 applications, and users' personal data sources, such as calendars, emails, chats, documents, meetings, and contacts. With natural language prompts, Business Chat can generate tailored responses, updates, or summaries based on the user's specific context and data. For example, a user could input "Tell my team how we updated the product strategy," and Business Chat would

analyze the user's recent meetings, emails, and chat threads to generate a comprehensive status update reflecting the latest product strategy discussions.

Copilot aims to streamline workflows, enhance productivity, and enable users to accomplish tasks more efficiently than ever before most especially when the existing Microsoft 365 applications are combined with the power of natural language processing and access to personal data. Microsoft Copilot represents a significant leap forward in how we interact with productivity software, leveraging the latest advances in artificial intelligence to augment and empower human capabilities.

Essentially, the following are salient points you need to know about on Microsoft Copilot:

- An AI-powered coding assistant that augments developers' efficiency.
- Employing machine learning algorithms to comprehend programming patterns.
- Generates code snippets, suggestions, and examples within the development environment.
- Seamlessly integrates with Visual Studio Code and GitHub's Copilot extension.
- Objective: Accelerate coding processes and facilitate high-quality code creation.
- Provides relevant documentation alongside code recommendations.
- Harnesses the potential of artificial intelligence to optimize development workflows.

- Enables developers to enhance productivity and streamline coding endeavors.
- Utilizes advanced techniques to understand and support programming practices.
- Aims to be an indispensable tool for efficient and effective software development.

Here's a simple guide to help you get started with Microsoft Copilot and set up your account:

1. Go to the Microsoft Copilot website at https://www.microsoft.com/en-us/copilot and click on the **"Sign Up"** button.

2. You will need to sign in using your Microsoft account. If you don't have one, you can easily create a new account by providing your email address and following the simple on-screen instructions.

3. After successfully logging in, you will be directed to the Microsoft Copilot dashboard. Here, you can carefully review the terms of service and privacy policy before proceeding by clicking **"Accept"**.

4. Now, it's time to establish your development environment. Microsoft Copilot currently offers support for Visual Studio Code and the GitHub

Copilot extension. Simply follow the prompts to install the required software and extensions.

5. Once you've successfully set up Visual Studio Code and added the GitHub Copilot extension, the next step is to authenticate your account within the extension. You can easily accomplish this by clicking on the Copilot icon in the Visual Studio Code sidebar and following the instructions displayed on the screen.

6. After successfully logging in, you can begin utilizing Microsoft Copilot in your coding projects. As you type, Copilot offers intelligent code suggestions, examples, and documentation tailored to your code context.

7. If you want to enhance your Copilot experience, you have the option to personalise it by modifying settings like suggestion behaviour, output formatting, and language preferences.

8. If you come across any problems or need help, you can consult the Microsoft Copilot documentation or contact their support team for assistance.

Keep in mind that the performance of Microsoft Copilot, an AI-powered tool, can vary based on the complexity of your code and the programming language you're using. Reviewing and understanding the generated code is crucial before incorporating it into your projects.

The AI Revolution and Its Impact

The rise of AI technology has ushered in a new era of innovation, disrupting traditional business models and creating unprecedented opportunities. As AI continues to evolve, its impact extends far beyond the realms of technology, driving transformative changes across industries and societies. Businesses that embrace AI gain a competitive edge by streamlining processes, enhancing decision-making, and delivering personalized experiences to customers. Individuals, too, can leverage AI to unlock new streams of income, automate tedious tasks, and enhance their skills and knowledge.

Copilot AI's Place in Microsoft's AI Ecosystem

Microsoft has long been at the forefront of technological innovation, and its commitment to AI is evident in the development of its robust AI ecosystem. Copilot AI seamlessly integrates with Microsoft's suite of products, including Microsoft 365, Azure AI, Designer, Teams, and the Power Platform, among others.

This integration enables users to harness the full potential of AI across various applications, from creating dynamic presentations and optimizing documents to developing compelling AI solutions and automating workflows. By leveraging Copilot AI in conjunction with Microsoft's other AI-powered tools, users can unlock a wealth of possibilities and drive innovation in their respective fields.

Key Features and Capabilities

Microsoft Copilot AI has a robust features and capabilities designed to enhance productivity, streamline workflows, and foster creativity. Some of its key offerings include:

1. **Natural Language Processing**: Copilot AI can understand and interpret human language, enabling users to communicate with the system using natural, conversational language.

2. **Content Generation**: Whether you need to draft documents, create presentations, or generate code, Copilot AI can assist you in producing high-quality content tailored to your specific needs.

3. **Data Analysis and Visualization**: With its advanced data processing capabilities, Copilot AI can analyze large datasets, identify patterns and insights, and present them in visually appealing and understandable formats.

4. **Task Automation**: By leveraging Copilot AI's automation capabilities, users can streamline repetitive tasks, freeing up time and resources for more strategic endeavors.

5. **Personalized Assistance**: Copilot AI can adapt to individual users' preferences and

workflows, providing personalized assistance and recommendations to enhance productivity and efficiency.

Microsoft 365: Elevating Collaboration and Productivity

A critical look at the modern business landscape shows that effective collaboration and productivity are essential for success. Microsoft 365 is a comprehensive suite of tools that empowers teams to work together seamlessly, regardless of their location or device. This powerful platform combines robust productivity applications with advanced communication and collaboration features, enabling businesses to streamline workflows and boost efficiency.

At the core of Microsoft 365 lies the familiar and widely-used Office applications, such as Word, Excel, PowerPoint, and Outlook. These industry-standard tools have been enhanced with cloud integration, allowing users to access and edit documents from anywhere, and collaborate in real-time with team members. Microsoft Teams, a central hub for communication and collaboration, seamlessly integrates with Office apps, enabling teams to share files, co-author documents, and engage in video conferences without ever leaving the platform.

One of the standout features of Microsoft 365 is its robust security and compliance capabilities. With built-in data protection, advanced threat protection, and compliance tools, businesses can safeguard their sensitive information and ensure adherence to industry regulations. This peace of mind allows teams to focus on their core tasks without worrying about data breaches or compliance issues.

Moreover, Microsoft 365 offers a range of productivity-enhancing tools and services. The AI-powered digital assistant, Cortana, can help users stay organized, manage tasks, and streamline workflows. Microsoft Planner and To-Do apps provide powerful project management and task tracking capabilities, ensuring that teams stay on top of their responsibilities and deadlines.

Azure AI: Harnessing the Power of Cloud AI

Businesses are increasingly turning to cloud-based solutions to harness the power of the contemporary transformative technology, especially in the present rapidly evolving world of artificial intelligence (AI). Microsoft Azure AI is a comprehensive suite of AI services and tools designed to help organizations accelerate their AI journey, from building and deploying models to managing and monitoring AI solutions at scale.

Azure AI offers a wide range of pre-built AI services, such as Computer Vision, Natural Language Processing (NLP), and Bot Services, enabling businesses to quickly incorporate AI capabilities into their applications and workflows. These services can be easily integrated with other Azure services, such as Azure Machine Learning and Azure Cognitive Services, to create end-to-end AI solutions tailored to specific business needs. One of the key advantages of Azure AI is its scalability and flexibility. With the power of the cloud, businesses can rapidly scale up or down their AI workloads as needed, ensuring optimal resource utilization and cost-effectiveness. Additionally, Azure AI provides a secure and compliant environment for AI workloads, ensuring that sensitive data and models are protected from unauthorized access.

Azure Machine Learning is a powerful tool within the Azure AI suite that enables data scientists and developers to build, train, and deploy machine learning models at scale. It offers a range of features, including automated machine learning, model management, and deployment pipelines, streamlining the entire lifecycle of machine learning projects.

Designer: Bringing Ideas to Life with AI-Powered Design

Design plays a crucial role in capturing attention and communicating ideas effectively. Microsoft Designer is an AI-powered design tool that empowers individuals and businesses to create stunning visuals with ease, regardless of their design expertise. Designer leverages advanced AI algorithms to understand the context and intent behind users' design requirements, providing intelligent suggestions and recommendations for layouts, images, colors, and fonts. This intelligent assistance not only saves time but also ensures that the final designs are visually appealing and consistent with industry best practices. One of the distinct features of Designer is its ability to create designs from scratch or enhance existing visuals. Users can simply provide a brief description or prompt, and Designer will generate a range of design options tailored to their needs. This feature is particularly useful for creating social media posts, presentations, marketing materials, and other design assets quickly and efficiently.

Designer also offers a vast library of professionally-designed templates, images, and graphics, ensuring that users have access to a wide range of high-quality design assets. These resources can be easily customized and integrated into the user's designs, saving valuable time and effort.

Teams: Streamlining Communication and Teamwork

Effective communication and collaboration are essential for driving productivity and success in the modern workplace. Microsoft Teams is a powerful platform that brings together various communication and collaboration tools into a single, unified environment, enabling teams to work seamlessly, regardless of their location. Teams provides a centralized hub for real-time messaging, video conferencing, and file sharing, allowing team members to stay connected and collaborate in real-time. The platform's intuitive interface and integration with other Microsoft 365 apps, such as Word, Excel, and PowerPoint, ensure a seamless user experience and streamlined workflows.

Teams has the ability to create dedicated channels for specific projects, topics, or teams. These channels serve as virtual workspaces, where team members can share files, engage in discussions, and collaborate on tasks. Additionally, Teams offers a range of collaboration tools, such as whiteboards, screen sharing, and co-authoring, enabling teams to work together effectively and efficiently. Teams also excels in facilitating external collaboration. Users can easily invite and collaborate with external partners, clients, or contractors, ensuring that everyone has access to the necessary information and resources. This feature is particularly valuable for businesses that frequently work with external stakeholders.

Power Platform: Automating Processes and Workflows

Streamlining procedures and automating workflows can greatly increase productivity and efficiency in the fast-paced commercial sector. With Microsoft Power Platform, businesses can easily create bespoke apps, automate workflows, and analyse data without requiring a deep understanding of code. It is a full set of low-code development tools. Power Platform has Power Apps, a no-code/low-code application development platform that allows users to create custom business applications quickly and easily. These applications can be designed to automate various processes, such as data entry, approval workflows, and task management, resulting in increased efficiency and productivity.

Power Automate is another powerful component of Power Platform, it enables users to create automated workflows and integrate them with various applications and services. This tool simplifies complex business processes by automating repetitive tasks, reducing manual effort, and minimizing the risk of errors.

Moreover, Power BI, Microsoft's business intelligence and data visualization tool, is also an integral part of Power Platform. With Power BI, users can easily connect to multiple data sources, transform and analyze data, and create interactive reports and dashboards that provide valuable insights for informed decision-making. The Power Platform ecosystem is further enhanced by its seamless integration with other Microsoft products and services, including Office 365, Dynamics 365, and Azure. This integration ensures a cohesive and seamless experience for users, enabling them to leverage the full potential of Microsoft's technology stack.

CHAPTER TWO

IDENTIFYING NICHE MARKETS AND CRAFTING AI SOLUTIONS

Understanding Niche Markets And Their Potential

Niche market identification and targeting has become a critical business strategy in the ever changing digital landscape. Niche markets are subsets of a broader market that have certain demands, wants, or interests in common. By serving these niche markets, business owners may set themselves apart from the competition and develop a devoted clientele. Niche markets present numerous advantages, including the ability to establish a strong brand identity, cultivate a dedicated customer base, and command premium pricing. By addressing the specific pain points and desires of a niche audience, businesses can deliver tailored solutions that resonate deeply with their target market, fostering customer loyalty and facilitating long-term growth.

Furthermore, niche markets often have a passionate and engaged community, which can serve as a valuable resource for market insights, product feedback, and word-of-mouth marketing. By immersing themselves in these communities, entrepreneurs can gain a deep understanding of their target audience's preferences, challenges, and aspirations, enabling them to refine their offerings and stay ahead of evolving trends.

Conducting Market Research and Analysis

Effective market research is the foundation for identifying and capitalizing on niche market opportunities. This process involves gathering and analyzing data to uncover valuable insights about the target market's demographics, behavior patterns, preferences, and pain points.

There are various methods to conduct market research, including online surveys, focus groups, interviews, and data analysis from industry reports and online forums. By leveraging these resources, entrepreneurs can gain a comprehensive understanding of the competitive landscape, consumer trends, and market gaps ripe for innovation. Analyzing the collected data is crucial for identifying patterns, trends, and emerging opportunities within the niche market. This analysis should encompass factors such as market size, growth potential, customer segmentation, and competitive dynamics. Additionally, entrepreneurs should assess the feasibility of implementing AI-powered solutions and their potential impact on addressing the identified market needs.

Ideating and Developing AI-Powered Solutions

Entrepreneurs can use AI technologies to generate ideas and create novel solutions if they possess a thorough understanding of the niche market and its particular difficulties. AI-powered solutions are ideally suited to meet the specific requirements of niche markets since they provide a host of benefits, such as increased efficiency, personalisation, and scalability.

Brainstorming sessions are an essential part of the ideation process, as they allow entrepreneurs to investigate different uses of AI and how they might improve current products or solve certain problems. At this stage, working with developers, domain experts, and AI experts may be necessary to guarantee the viability and efficacy of the suggested solutions. Once the initial ideas have been generated, the development phase begins. This involves translating the concepts into tangible AI-powered products or services. Depending on the nature of the solution, this may involve integrating AI algorithms, machine learning models, natural language processing (NLP) capabilities, or other cutting-edge technologies.

Validating and Testing Your AI Solution

Before launching an AI-powered solution, it is important to validate and test its effectiveness, usability, and potential impact on the target niche market. This process helps identify and address any potential issues or shortcomings, ensuring that the solution meets the desired standards and delivers value to the intended audience.

Validation can be achieved through various methods, such as conducting pilot studies, beta testing, or gathering feedback from a sample of the target market. By involving potential customers in the validation process, entrepreneurs can gain valuable insights and refine their solutions to better align with the market's needs and preferences.

To guarantee the accuracy, dependability, and scalability of the AI system, extensive testing is also necessary. This could entail stress testing, scenario modelling, and performance analysis of the solution under various conditions. By fixing any faults or issues found at this stage, future difficulties can be avoided and the user experience can be improved overall.

Pivoting and Refining Your Approach

Despite thorough research and planning, it is not uncommon for entrepreneurs to encounter challenges or unforeseen circumstances when introducing an AI-powered solution to a niche market. In such situations, it is essential to remain agile and open to pivoting and refining the approach. Pivoting involves making strategic changes to the product, service, or business model based on feedback, market trends, or emerging opportunities. This may involve adjusting the target audience, modifying the AI solution's features, or exploring alternative revenue streams or partnerships.

Continuous refinement is also crucial to ensure that the AI-powered solution remains relevant and competitive in the ever-changing market landscape. This may involve incorporating new AI technologies, updating algorithms, or adapting to evolving customer preferences and industry trends.

By embracing a mindset of continuous improvement and adaptation, entrepreneurs can stay ahead of the curve, maintain a competitive edge, and continue to deliver value to their niche market.

CHAPTER THREE

BUILDING A SUSTAINABLE ONLINE BUSINESS

Developing A Solid Business Plan

Crafting a comprehensive and well-thought-out business plan is crucial for any online venture's success. It serves as a roadmap, guiding you through the intricate process of establishing and growing your digital enterprise. A robust business plan should encompass several key elements, including a detailed market analysis, a thorough understanding of your target audience, a compelling value proposition, and a strategic marketing plan.

Begin by conducting extensive research into your chosen industry, identifying potential competitors, and pinpointing untapped market opportunities. This will not only help you differentiate your offerings but also enable you to tailor your products or services to meet the specific needs of your target customers. Additionally, a comprehensive market analysis will provide valuable insights into pricing strategies, distribution channels, and potential obstacles or challenges you may encounter along the way.

Next, clearly define your unique value proposition – the distinctive benefit or advantage that sets your online business apart from the competition. This could be a innovative product or service, a superior customer experience, or a niche market focus. Articulating your value proposition will help you craft a compelling brand narrative and resonate with your target audience.

Furthermore, a solid business plan should outline your marketing strategies, including digital marketing tactics, social media campaigns, and potential partnerships or collaborations. This will not only help you attract and retain customers but also establish a strong online presence and build brand awareness.

Finally, incorporate financial projections, including startup costs, operational expenses, revenue forecasts, and potential funding sources. This will not only ensure you have the necessary resources to launch and sustain your online business but also provide a framework for monitoring your financial performance and making data-driven decisions.

Securing Funding and Investments

Launching and growing an online business often requires

substantial financial resources, particularly in the early stages. Therefore, securing funding and investments should be a top priority for aspiring entrepreneurs. There are various avenues to explore, each with its own advantages and considerations.

One popular option is seeking investment from angel investors or venture capitalists. These individuals or firms specialize in providing capital to promising startups in exchange for equity or ownership stakes. While this route can provide substantial funding, it also involves relinquishing some control over your business and adhering to the investors' expectations and governance.

Alternatively, crowdfunding platforms have emerged as a viable source of funding for online businesses. These platforms allow entrepreneurs to pitch their ideas and products directly to potential backers, who can contribute funds in exchange for rewards or equity shares. Successful crowdfunding campaigns not only provide financial backing but also validate the market demand for your offerings.

Traditional lending institutions, such as banks or credit unions, may also offer business loans or lines of credit. While these options typically require collateral and a strong credit history, they allow you to maintain full ownership and control over your online venture.

Additionally, explore government-sponsored grants or

programs designed to support small businesses and entrepreneurs. These initiatives often provide funding, resources, and mentorship opportunities, particularly for underrepresented or marginalized groups.

Regardless of the funding source you pursue, it is essential to present a compelling business plan, demonstrating the viability and growth potential of your online business. Investors and lenders alike will scrutinize your financial projections, market analysis, and strategies for generating revenue and achieving profitability.

Scaling and Growing Your Online Business

As your online business gains traction and establishes a solid customer base, it's crucial to have a well-defined strategy for scaling and growth. This will not only ensure you can meet increasing demand but also position your venture for long-term success and sustainability. One of the key aspects of scaling is optimizing your operational processes and workflows. Streamlining tasks, automating repetitive activities, and leveraging technology solutions can significantly improve efficiency and productivity, enabling you to handle a larger volume of orders or clients without compromising quality or customer service. Expanding your product or service offerings can also drive growth and attract new customer segments. Conduct market research, gather customer feedback, and identify emerging trends or unmet needs within your industry. This will allow you to diversify your revenue streams and strengthen your competitive position.

In addition, consider exploring new distribution channels or partnerships to reach wider audiences. Collaborating with complementary businesses, influencers, or industry experts can open up new marketing avenues and amplify your brand's reach. As you scale, it's crucial to maintain a consistent and exceptional customer experience. Invest in robust customer support systems, implement quality control measures, and continuously gather feedback to identify areas for improvement. A strong reputation for outstanding service can be a powerful differentiator and driver of growth.

Finally, be prepared to adapt and pivot as your online business evolves. Regularly review your strategies, monitor industry trends, and remain agile in your approach. Embracing change and innovation will enable you to capitalize on new opportunities and stay ahead of the competition.

Managing Resources and Finances

Effective resource and financial management is vital for the long-term sustainability and profitability of any online business. It involves carefully monitoring and optimizing various aspects of your operations, from cash flow and budgeting to inventory management and cost control.

Start by implementing robust financial tracking and reporting systems. Regularly analyze your income statements, balance sheets, and cash flow statements to gain insights into your business's financial health and identify areas for improvement or potential cost-saving opportunities. Cash flow management is particularly crucial for online businesses, as it ensures you have sufficient liquidity to cover operational expenses, invest in growth initiatives, and navigate any unexpected challenges. Develop strategies for managing accounts receivable and payable, and consider implementing invoicing and payment processing solutions that streamline these processes.

Inventory management is another critical aspect, especially for e-commerce businesses or those offering physical products. Implement systems to track stock levels, monitor sales patterns, and optimize inventory levels to minimize carrying costs while ensuring you can meet customer demand. Also, regularly review and negotiate with suppliers, vendors, and service providers to secure favorable terms and pricing. Leverage your purchasing power and explore opportunities for bulk discounts or long-term contracts. When it comes to managing human resources, prioritize efficiency and productivity. Implement performance management systems, provide training and development opportunities, and foster a culture of continuous improvement. Automating processes and leveraging technology solutions can also help optimize your workforce and reduce labor costs.

Regularly review and adjust your pricing strategies to ensure you are generating adequate profit margins while remaining competitive. Conduct market research, analyze customer behavior and willingness to pay, and consider implementing dynamic pricing models or offering bundled packages or subscriptions.

Building a Strong Brand and Online Presence

Building a strong brand and online presence is crucial for drawing in and keeping customers, establishing trust, and encouraging loyalty in the crowded and always changing digital market. A strong brand strategy may help you stand out from the competition, communicate your special selling point, and connect with your target market.

Start by defining your brand's core values, personality, and messaging. These elements should align with your business's mission, vision, and the needs and preferences of your target customers. Consistency across all touchpoints, from your website and social media profiles to your marketing materials and customer interactions, is key to reinforcing your brand identity. Develop a visually appealing and user-friendly website that serves as the foundation of your online presence. Ensure it is optimized for search engines, mobile-responsive, and seamlessly integrates with your e-commerce platform or lead generation strategies. Additionally, consider incorporating multimedia content, such as videos, infographics, or podcasts, to engage your audience and establish thought leadership within your industry.

Make smart use of social media platforms to engage with your audience, develop a sense of community around your online business, and increase brand exposure. Contribute insightful information, engage with your audience, and take part in pertinent industry debates and conversations. Strategic alliances and influencer marketing are other ways to expand your audience and establish trust.

Building a solid online presence also requires managing your internet reputation. Keep an eye on and react to customer evaluations, deal with any unfavourable comments in a timely and professional manner, and actively seek out and present success stories and endorsements. And lastly, look at content marketing opportunities like guest posting, blogging, and contributing to trade journals. Establish credibility, draw in organic traffic, and create enduring bonds with your target audience by presenting yourself and your company online as a reliable authority in your industry.

CHAPTER FOUR

MARKETING STRATEGIES FOR AI PRODUCTS AND SERVICES

Understanding The Ai Market Landscape

The market for artificial intelligence is growing rapidly due to technological breakthroughs and the rising need for intelligent solutions in a variety of industries. A thorough grasp of the market landscape is essential for marketing your AI goods and services. This entails assessing the competitive environment, seeing new trends, and appreciating the special difficulties and possibilities present in the AI ecosystem.

Begin by conducting thorough market research to gain insights into the current state of the AI market. Analyze the key players, their offerings, and their positioning strategies. Identify the gaps and unmet needs that your AI solution can address. Additionally, stay updated on the latest technological advancements, regulatory changes, and consumer preferences that could impact the adoption and perception of AI solutions. Also, it's essential to understand the specific industry or domain in which your AI product or service operates. Each industry has its own challenges, pain points, and customer expectations. By developing a comprehensive understanding of the industry dynamics, you can tailor your marketing strategies and messaging to resonate with your target audience effectively.

Crafting Compelling Marketing Campaigns

Understanding the dynamics of the AI market is crucial for creating impactful marketing campaigns that will grab the attention of your desired audience and set your products apart from the competition. Begin by clearly defining your unique value proposition - the key benefits and advantages that differentiate your AI solution from competitors. These factors could encompass superior performance, enhanced efficiency, cost-effectiveness, or innovative features.

Once you have identified your unique value proposition, develop a cohesive and consistent brand identity that reflects your AI solution's strengths and aligns with your target audience's preferences. This includes creating a compelling brand story, visual identity, and messaging that resonates with your target customers. Utilize various marketing channels to reach your target audience effectively. This may include a combination of traditional marketing tactics, such as print and broadcast advertising, as well as digital marketing strategies, including search engine optimization (SEO), pay-per-click (PPC) advertising, social media marketing, and email marketing campaigns.

Leveraging Social Media and Influencer Marketing

Social media and influencer marketing have become powerful tools for promoting AI products and services. With the increasing use of social media platforms, leveraging these channels can help you reach and engage with your target audience more effectively.

Develop a strong social media presence by creating and maintaining active profiles on relevant platforms. Share valuable content, engage with your audience, and leverage social media advertising to amplify your reach. Additionally, consider partnering with influencers in the AI and technology space who have a strong following and credibility within your target market.

Influencer marketing can be particularly effective for AI products and services, as it can help build trust and credibility with potential customers. Identify influencers who align with your brand values and target audience, and collaborate with them to promote your AI solution through sponsored content, product reviews, or brand ambassadorship.

Content Marketing and Thought Leadership

Content marketing and thought leadership are crucial components of an effective marketing strategy for AI products and services. By creating and sharing valuable, educational, and informative content, you can position your brand as a trusted authority in the AI space and build a strong relationship with your target audience.

Develop a content marketing strategy that aligns with your target audience's interests and pain points. This may include creating blog posts, whitepapers, case studies, infographics, webinars, and video content that educates and informs your audience about the benefits and applications of your AI solution.

Additionally, participate in industry events, conferences, and online communities to share your expertise and establish yourself as a thought leader in the AI field. This can help increase brand awareness, build credibility, and position your AI solution as a go-to option for businesses seeking innovative and effective solutions.

Measuring and Optimizing Your Marketing Efforts

Measuring and optimizing your marketing efforts is crucial for ensuring the success of your AI product or service. Establish clear Key Performance Indicators (KPIs) that align with your marketing objectives, such as website traffic, lead generation, conversion rates, and customer acquisition costs.

Implement analytics tools and tracking mechanisms to monitor and analyze the performance of your marketing campaigns across various channels. This will provide valuable insights into what's working and what needs improvement, allowing you to make data-driven decisions and optimize your marketing strategies accordingly.

Regularly review and analyze your marketing performance data, and make necessary adjustments to your campaigns, messaging, and targeting. A/B testing can be an effective way to test different marketing approaches and identify the most effective strategies for your target audience.

Take a note that marketing is an iterative process, and continuous optimization is key to staying ahead in the competitive AI market. By consistently measuring and refining your marketing efforts, you can ensure that your AI product or service remains visible, relevant, and attractive to your target customers.

CHAPTER FIVE

UNDERSTANDING COPILOT AI'S CAPABILITIES

Natural Language Processing And Conversational Ai

Artificial Intelligence (AI) has made remarkable strides in the realm of Natural Language Processing (NLP) and conversational AI. NLP is a branch of AI that deals with the interaction between computers and humans using natural language. It aims to enable machines to understand, interpret, and generate human-like speech and text.

Conversational AI is an application of NLP that allows computers to engage in natural, human-like conversations. It involves understanding the context, intent, and sentiment behind a user's input, and providing relevant and coherent responses. This technology has revolutionized the way we interact with digital assistants, chatbots, and virtual agents.

One of the key advantages of conversational AI is its ability to comprehend and communicate in multiple languages. It can analyze and respond to user inputs in various dialects and regional variations, making it accessible to a global audience. Additionally, conversational AI can learn and adapt to individual communication styles, providing a personalized and seamless experience.

Furthermore, conversational AI has found applications in diverse domains such as customer service, healthcare, education, and e-commerce. Virtual assistants can handle customer inquiries, provide product recommendations, and assist with task completion, significantly enhancing the user experience and operational efficiency.

Text Generation and Content Creation

AI has made significant strides in text generation and content creation, enabling machines to produce human-like written output. This capability has numerous applications, ranging from creative writing and article generation to document summarization and translation.

One of the key technologies driving text generation is natural language generation (NLG). NLG algorithms analyze structured data and convert it into coherent and fluent text, mimicking human writing styles. This technology has found applications in report generation, content personalization, and data storytelling, enabling businesses to communicate complex information effectively.

Another area where AI excels is content creation. AI-powered writing assistants can generate high-quality content on various topics, from blog posts and product descriptions to marketing materials and academic papers. These assistants can understand prompts, conduct research, and synthesize information to produce engaging and informative content.

Furthermore, AI can be used to enhance existing content by suggesting improvements, detecting and correcting errors, and optimizing for readability and search engine optimization (SEO). This not only saves time and effort but also ensures consistency and quality across various content types.

Data Analysis and Visualization

AI has revolutionized the way we analyze and visualize data. With the ability to process vast amounts of data quickly and accurately, AI algorithms can uncover hidden patterns, trends, and insights that would be difficult or impossible for humans to detect manually.

One of the key applications of AI in data analysis is predictive modeling. By leveraging machine learning techniques, AI can analyze historical data and identify patterns to make accurate predictions about future events or outcomes. This has wide-ranging applications in areas such as sales forecasting, risk assessment, and fraud detection.

AI also plays a crucial role in data visualization, helping to present complex data in a clear and intuitive manner. AI algorithms can automatically generate visualizations such as charts, graphs, and infographics, tailored to the specific data and audience. These visualizations can aid in data exploration, communication, and decision-making processes.

Furthermore, AI can enhance data visualization by providing interactive and dynamic capabilities. For example, users can ask natural language questions about the data, and AI-powered systems can generate relevant visualizations and insights on the fly, facilitating a more immersive and insightful data exploration experience.

Task Automation and Process Optimization

AI has the potential to automate a wide range of tasks and processes, leading to increased efficiency, productivity, and cost savings. By leveraging machine learning algorithms and robotic process automation (RPA), AI can learn and mimic human actions, automating repetitive and time-consuming tasks with high accuracy and consistency.

One area where task automation has gained significant traction is in business process optimization. AI can analyze existing processes, identify bottlenecks and inefficiencies, and recommend optimizations or automate specific tasks within the process. This can lead to streamlined operations, reduced operational costs, and improved customer experiences.

In addition to process optimization, AI can automate a variety of tasks across various industries. For example, in finance and accounting, AI can automate invoice processing, data entry, and financial report generation. In healthcare, AI can assist with medical image analysis, patient triage, and appointment scheduling. In manufacturing, AI can optimize production lines, predict equipment failures, and ensure quality control.

Furthermore, AI-powered virtual assistants and chatbots can automate customer service tasks, providing 24/7 support and handling routine inquiries, freeing up human agents to focus on more complex issues. This not only improves customer satisfaction but also reduces operational costs associated with traditional customer service channels.

AI-Powered Coding and Development

AI has made significant advancements in the field of software development, offering tools and capabilities that can streamline the coding and development process. AI-powered coding assistants can analyze code, identify errors, suggest improvements, and even generate code snippets based on natural language prompts.

One of the key benefits of AI-powered coding is its ability to enhance code quality and maintainability. AI algorithms can analyze code for potential issues such as security vulnerabilities, performance bottlenecks, and code smells, providing recommendations for improvements. This not only reduces the likelihood of bugs and errors but also ensures that the codebase adheres to best practices and industry standards.

Additionally, AI can assist in code generation and automation. By understanding natural language prompts and specifications, AI-powered tools can generate code for various tasks such as web development, mobile app development, and data processing pipelines. This can significantly accelerate the development process and reduce the time and effort required for coding.

Furthermore, AI can aid in code comprehension and documentation. By analyzing existing codebases, AI algorithms can generate summaries, documentation, and explanations, making it easier for developers to understand and maintain complex systems.

AI-powered development environments can also provide real-time assistance and recommendations based on the developer's coding patterns and preferences. This personalized support can enhance productivity and enable developers to focus on more creative and strategic aspects of software development.

CHAPTER SIX

CONTENT CREATION AND COPILOT AI

Writing Engaging Blog Posts And Articles

In today's digital age, crafting compelling content is essential for establishing a robust online presence and connecting with your audience. Crafting high-quality blog posts and articles is essential for success, regardless of whether you're a blogger, a content creator, or a business owner. Utilizing Microsoft Copilot AI, you can enhance your writing skills and create content that deeply connects with your audience.

Copilot AI can assist you in various aspects of the content creation process, from generating ideas and structuring your thoughts to refining your writing style and ensuring grammatical accuracy. By leveraging its natural language processing capabilities, Copilot AI can provide you with relevant insights, suggestions, and recommendations tailored to your specific needs. One of the key benefits of using Copilot AI for writing blog posts and articles is its ability to streamline the ideation process. By providing you with prompts and inspiration, Copilot AI can help you overcome writer's block and spark creativity. Additionally, it can assist you in conducting research, gathering relevant information, and organizing your thoughts into a cohesive structure.

When it comes to crafting engaging content, Copilot AI can help you strike the right tone and maintain a consistent voice throughout your writing. It can suggest word choices, sentence structures, and stylistic elements that align with your target audience and the intended message. Furthermore, Copilot AI can analyze your writing for clarity, conciseness, and overall readability, ensuring that your content is easy to understand and engaging for your readers.

Crafting Compelling Sales Copy

When it comes to the realm of marketing and advertising, creating persuasive sales copy is truly an art form. Having well-crafted sales copy is crucial for the success of your product descriptions, landing pages, and email campaigns. Using Microsoft Copilot AI, you can enhance your copywriting abilities and create sales copy that deeply connects with your intended audience. Copilot AI can assist you in various aspects of the copywriting process, from understanding your target audience and their pain points to crafting persuasive messaging that speaks directly to their needs and desires. By leveraging its natural language processing capabilities, Copilot AI can provide you with insights and recommendations tailored to your specific marketing goals.

One of the key benefits of using Copilot AI for crafting sales copy is its ability to help you understand your target audience on a deeper level. By analyzing data and customer feedback, Copilot AI can provide you with valuable insights into your audience's preferences, behaviors, and motivations. Armed with this knowledge, you can craft sales copy that speaks directly to their pain points and addresses their specific needs and desires. Copilot AI can also assist you in developing a strong value proposition and crafting persuasive messaging that sets your product or service apart from the competition. It can suggest attention-grabbing headlines, compelling call-to-actions, and persuasive language that resonates with your target audience and motivates them to take action.

Developing Instructional and Training Materials

Delivering impactful training and instruction is essential for driving the success of your organization and its employees in today's dynamic business landscape. When it comes to developing training materials for new hires, creating instructional manuals for customers, or designing online courses, the quality of your content plays a crucial role in shaping the learning experience and enhancing knowledge retention. With Microsoft Copilot AI, you can revolutionize the way you develop instructional and training materials, ensuring that your content is engaging, informative, and tailored to the specific needs of your audience. Copilot AI can assist you in various aspects of the content creation process, from structuring and organizing your material to ensuring clarity and accuracy.

One of the key benefits of using Copilot AI for developing instructional and training materials is its ability to help you break down complex topics into easily digestible chunks. By leveraging its natural language processing capabilities, Copilot AI can analyze your content and provide suggestions for breaking it down into logical sections, ensuring that your audience can follow along and absorb the information effectively.

Also, Copilot AI can assist you in creating engaging and interactive content that keeps your audience engaged and motivated to learn. It can suggest multimedia elements, such as videos, animations, and interactive quizzes, that reinforce key concepts and ensure better knowledge retention. Additionally, Copilot AI can help you tailor your content to different learning styles, ensuring that your materials cater to a diverse audience.

Generating Social Media Content

In today's digital era, social media has emerged as a potent tool for businesses, influencers, and individuals to establish a robust online presence and engage with their target audience. Creating engaging and relevant social media content can be quite challenging. It requires a lot of creativity, strategic planning, and a thorough understanding of your target audience. With Microsoft Copilot AI, you can streamline the process of generating social media content and ensure that your posts resonate with your followers, driving engagement and building a loyal community. Copilot AI can assist you in various aspects of social media content creation, from ideation and planning to execution and optimization. One of the key benefits of using Copilot AI for generating social media content is its ability to help you understand your audience's preferences and behaviors. By analyzing data from your social media channels, Copilot AI can provide you with valuable insights into what type of content resonates best with your followers, when they are most active, and which platforms they prefer.

If this is taken into consideration, Copilot AI can be used in creating a comprehensive social media content strategy that aligns with your goals and resonates with your target audience. It can suggest content themes, formats, and schedules that maximize engagement and ensure a consistent brand presence across all your social media channels.

AI-Assisted Copywriting and Editing

Today, effective communication is essential for achieving success in any industry. If you want to excel in creating marketing materials, business proposals, or website content, the way you write plays a crucial role in connecting with your audience and effectively conveying your message.

With Microsoft Copilot AI, you can elevate your copywriting and editing skills, ensuring that your content is polished, engaging, and tailored to your specific needs. Copilot AI can assist you in various aspects of the writing and editing process, from ideation and structure to style and grammar. Copilot AI helps you to streamline the writing process and improve your productivity. By leveraging its natural language processing capabilities, Copilot AI can provide you with suggestions for word choice, sentence structure, and overall flow, ensuring that your writing is clear, concise, and engaging.

Moreover, AI can also assist you in ensuring consistency and adherence to brand guidelines and style guides. It can analyze your content for tone, voice, and messaging, providing recommendations to ensure that your writing aligns with your brand identity and resonates with your target audience. In addition to copywriting assistance, Copilot AI can be a powerful tool for editing and proofreading. It can identify grammatical errors, spelling mistakes, and stylistic inconsistencies, ensuring that your content is polished and professional. Furthermore, Copilot AI can provide suggestions for improving readability, clarity, and overall impact, helping you to craft content that truly resonates with your audience.

CHAPTER SEVEN

DATA ANALYSIS WITH COPILOT AI

Extracting Insights From Complex Datasets

The world is now a data-driven one. Thus, businesses are inundated with vast amounts of complex information from multiple sources. Navigating these intricate datasets can be a daunting task, but Microsoft's Copilot AI offers a powerful solution. With its advanced natural language processing capabilities, Copilot AI can quickly comprehend and analyze even the most convoluted data, extracting valuable insights that would be challenging for humans to discern. Ability to identify patterns, trends, and correlations within large datasets is one of the standout features of Copilot AI. By leveraging machine learning algorithms and deep neural networks, the AI can sift through millions of data points, recognizing subtle relationships and anomalies that may have gone unnoticed by traditional analytical methods.

Moreover, Copilot AI excels at handling unstructured data, such as text documents, images, and audio files. It can process and interpret this information, transforming it into structured, quantifiable data that can be seamlessly integrated into existing business intelligence systems.

Building Interactive Data Visualizations

Effective data visualization is crucial for conveying complex information in a clear and compelling manner. Copilot AI offers a range of tools and features that enable businesses to create stunning, interactive visualizations that bring their data to life. With natural language prompts, users can instruct Copilot AI to generate customized charts, graphs, and dashboards that accurately depict the desired data. These visualizations can be tailored to specific audiences, ensuring that the information is presented in a way that resonates with the intended viewers.

One of the key advantages of Copilot AI's data visualization capabilities is its ability to integrate with Microsoft's suite of productivity tools, such as PowerPoint and Excel. This seamless integration allows users to effortlessly incorporate their visualizations into presentations, reports, and other business documents, streamlining the communication process.

Forecasting and Predictive Modeling

The ability to anticipate future trends and make informed

decisions is invaluable in business landscape. Copilot AI's forecasting and predictive modeling capabilities empower organizations to stay ahead of the curve by leveraging historical data and advanced algorithms. By analyzing patterns and relationships within existing datasets, Copilot AI can develop sophisticated predictive models that forecast future outcomes with remarkable accuracy. These models can be applied to various business scenarios, such as sales forecasting, resource planning, and risk assessment, providing decision-makers with crucial insights for strategic planning.

Furthermore, Copilot AI's continuous learning capabilities ensure that these predictive models are constantly updated and refined as new data becomes available. This adaptive approach ensures that businesses can make decisions based on the most current and relevant information, minimizing the risk of relying on outdated or inaccurate projections.

Automating Routine Data Tasks

Data analysis often involves a significant amount of repetitive, time-consuming tasks, such as data cleaning, formatting, and transformation. Copilot AI offers a solution to this challenge by automating these routine processes, freeing up valuable time and resources for more critical analytical endeavors. With the use of natural language prompts, users can instruct Copilot AI to perform a wide range of data manipulation tasks, from merging and filtering datasets to applying complex calculations and transformations. These automated processes not only save time but also reduce the risk of human error, ensuring the integrity and accuracy of the data being analyzed.

Moreover, Copilot AI's automation capabilities can be seamlessly integrated into existing workflows and business processes, enabling organizations to streamline their data operations and increase overall efficiency.

Integrating AI with Business Intelligence Tools

While Copilot AI is a powerful data analysis tool in its own right, its true potential is realized when integrated with other business intelligence solutions. Microsoft's ecosystem of productivity and analytics tools, such as Power BI and SQL Server, provides a robust foundation for leveraging Copilot AI's capabilities. By combining the advanced features of these tools with Copilot AI's natural language processing and machine learning capabilities, businesses can unlock new levels of insight and productivity. For example, users can seamlessly incorporate Copilot AI's predictive models into Power BI dashboards, enabling real-time monitoring and decision-making based on up-to-date forecasts.

Furthermore, the integration of Copilot AI with SQL Server and other database management systems allows for efficient querying and analysis of large, complex datasets, empowering businesses to make data-driven decisions with unprecedented speed and accuracy. Microsoft's Copilot AI offers a comprehensive solution for businesses seeking to harness the power of data analysis and gain a competitive edge. From extracting insights from complex datasets to building interactive visualizations and automating routine tasks, Copilot AI provides a versatile toolkit for unlocking the full potential of data-driven decision-making.

CHAPTER EIGHT

PROCESS AUTOMATION AND WORKFLOWS

Streamlining Administrative And Office Tasks

Administrative tasks can be a major drain on an organization's resources in today's fast-paced business environment. By harnessing the power of cutting-edge AI technologies, companies can optimize these processes, allowing them to save precious time and resources. One area where AI can make a significant impact is in document management. Intelligent document processing systems can automatically classify, extract, and organize data from various sources, eliminating the need for manual data entry and filing. These systems can also assist with tasks such as document generation, template creation, and version control, ensuring consistency and accuracy across all documentation. Another area where AI can be invaluable is in scheduling and calendar management.

AI-powered virtual assistants can intelligently manage appointments, schedule meetings, and coordinate with team members, minimizing scheduling conflicts and ensuring efficient use of time.

AI can also play a crucial role in automating routine office tasks such as email management, data entry, and report generation. By leveraging natural language processing and machine learning algorithms, AI systems can intelligently categorize and prioritize emails, automatically populate data fields, and generate customized reports based on specific criteria.

Automating Customer Service and Support

AI has the potential to completely transform the way businesses engage with their customers in the realm of customer service and support. Intelligent chatbots and virtual assistants are capable of offering round-the-clock support, addressing common inquiries, resolving problems, and delivering tailored suggestions. These AI-powered systems can be trained on vast knowledge bases, ensuring that they can provide accurate and consistent responses to a wide range of customer inquiries. Additionally, they can leverage natural language processing and sentiment analysis to understand the context and intent behind customer queries, enabling more meaningful and personalized interactions.

By automating routine customer service tasks, AI can significantly reduce response times and improve overall customer satisfaction. This not only enhances the customer experience but also frees up human agents to focus on more complex and high-value interactions.

Optimizing Project Management Processes

Project management is a complex and multifaceted process that involves coordinating various resources, tasks, and stakeholders. AI can play a pivotal role in optimizing these processes, improving efficiency, and increasing the likelihood of successful project delivery. One area where AI can make a significant impact is in task scheduling and resource allocation. By leveraging machine learning algorithms and constraint optimization techniques, AI systems can intelligently assign tasks to team members based on their skills, availability, and workload, ensuring optimal utilization of resources. Also, AI assists in project risk management by analyzing historical data, identifying potential risks, and providing proactive mitigation strategies. These systems can continuously monitor project progress, detect deviations from planned timelines or budgets, and alert project managers to potential issues before they escalate.

Furthermore, AI-powered collaboration tools can facilitate seamless communication and coordination among team members, enabling real-time updates, document sharing, and task tracking. These tools can leverage natural language processing to interpret and summarize meeting notes, action items, and project updates, ensuring that all stakeholders remain aligned and informed.

Integrating AI into Existing Workflows

While AI holds immense potential for process automation and workflow optimization, seamlessly integrating these technologies into existing systems and processes is crucial for maximizing their impact. Organizations must carefully assess their current workflows, identify areas for improvement, and develop a strategic plan for AI integration. One approach is to start small by implementing AI solutions in specific, well-defined processes or departments. This allows organizations to evaluate the effectiveness of the AI system, gather user feedback, and make necessary adjustments before scaling to other areas of the business.

It is also essential to ensure that AI solutions are seamlessly integrated with existing software and systems. This may involve leveraging APIs, developing custom integrations, or implementing AI platforms that can easily interface with various applications and data sources. Successful AI integration also requires a robust change management strategy. Organizations must provide adequate training and support to employees, addressing any concerns or resistance to the adoption of new technologies. Fostering a culture of continuous learning and embracing innovation can significantly facilitate the smooth integration of AI into existing workflows.

Building Custom AI-Powered Solutions

If organizations have unique requirements or specialized processes, they may need to develop custom AI-powered solutions, even though there are many off-the-shelf AI solutions available. When faced with such situations, it becomes crucial to work together with experts in AI, data science, and software development. The first step in building a custom AI solution is to clearly define the problem or process that needs to be optimized. This involves a thorough analysis of current workflows, data sources, and stakeholder requirements. By understanding the specific challenges and goals, the development team can design an AI solution tailored to the organization's needs. Then, the team must gather and prepare the necessary data to train the AI models. This may involve collecting and cleaning data from various sources, such as databases, documents, or digital assets. Ensuring data quality and completeness is crucial for developing accurate and reliable AI models.

Once the data is prepared, the development team can begin building and training the AI models using various machine learning techniques, such as supervised learning, unsupervised learning, or reinforcement learning, depending on the specific requirements of the solution. Throughout the development process, it is important to continuously test and evaluate the AI solution, gathering feedback from end-users and stakeholders. This iterative approach ensures that the final product meets the organization's needs and delivers the desired outcomes.

Finally, the custom AI solution must be integrated into the existing workflows and systems, requiring careful planning, testing, and implementation strategies. Ongoing monitoring, maintenance, and updates are also essential to ensure the AI solution remains effective and adaptable to changing business requirements.

CHAPTER NINE

AI-POWERED CODING AND DEVELOPMENT

Code Generation And Assistance

Artificial Intelligence (AI) has revolutionized the coding and development landscape, offering unprecedented opportunities for streamlining processes and enhancing productivity. Code generation and assistance tools powered by AI are designed to alleviate the burden of tedious and repetitive tasks, allowing developers to focus on more complex and creative aspects of their work. One of the most significant advantages of AI-assisted code generation is its ability to rapidly produce boilerplate code, which forms the foundation for various software applications. By leveraging AI algorithms trained on vast repositories of existing code, these tools can generate high-quality, functional code snippets tailored to specific requirements. This not only saves developers countless hours of manual coding but also reduces the likelihood of human errors, leading to more robust and reliable applications.

Moreover, AI-driven code assistance features, such as intelligent code completion and real-time error detection, have become indispensable for modern developers. These features analyze the context of the code being written and provide intelligent suggestions, reducing the cognitive load on developers and enabling them to write code more efficiently and accurately. AI-powered code generation and assistance tools can seamlessly integrate with existing development environments, offering a natural and intuitive experience for developers. By understanding natural language inputs, these tools can interpret developers' intentions and translate them into executable code, bridging the gap between human thought processes and machine-readable instructions.

AI-Driven Software Testing and Debugging

Software testing and debugging are critical phases in the development lifecycle, ensuring the quality and reliability of applications. AI has emerged as a powerful ally in these processes, offering innovative techniques to identify and address defects more effectively. AI-driven software testing leverages machine learning algorithms to analyze vast amounts of data, including code repositories, test results, and user feedback. By identifying patterns and anomalies, AI can generate comprehensive test cases and scenarios tailored to the specific application, increasing the likelihood of catching bugs and edge cases that may have been overlooked by traditional testing methods.

Furthermore, AI can assist in the debugging process by analyzing error logs, stack traces, and code repositories to pinpoint the root cause of issues more quickly. Intelligent debugging tools can suggest potential solutions, highlight similar issues encountered in other projects, and even propose code fixes, significantly reducing the time and effort required for resolving defects. AI-powered testing and debugging tools can also adapt and learn from the results of their analyses, continuously improving their accuracy and effectiveness over time. This iterative learning process ensures that the tools remain relevant and valuable as software systems evolve and become more complex.

Rapid Prototyping and Iterative Development

Agile methodologies and iterative development approaches have become the norm in modern software engineering practices. AI technologies can significantly enhance these processes by enabling rapid prototyping and facilitating continuous iterations. AI-driven prototyping tools can quickly generate functional prototypes based on high-level specifications or user requirements. These prototypes can then be refined and iterated upon through continuous feedback cycles, allowing developers to validate their assumptions, gather user insights, and make informed decisions about the product's direction.

Moreover, AI can assist in the iterative development process by analyzing user feedback, market trends, and performance metrics. This data-driven approach allows developers to prioritize features, identify areas for improvement, and make informed decisions about future iterations, ensuring that the product remains aligned with user needs and market demands.

By streamlining the prototyping and iterative development processes, AI empowers teams to deliver high-quality, user-centric software solutions more efficiently and effectively, fostering a culture of continuous improvement and innovation.

Integrating AI into Existing Applications

While AI technologies are revolutionizing the way software is developed, they can also be seamlessly integrated into existing applications to enhance their capabilities and provide added value to end-users. AI-powered features, such as natural language processing (NLP), computer vision, and predictive analytics, can be embedded into existing applications to enable more intuitive and intelligent user experiences. For example, NLP can facilitate conversational interfaces, allowing users to interact with applications using natural language commands and queries.

Moreover, AI can be leveraged to personalize user experiences by analyzing usage patterns, preferences, and historical data. Personalized recommendations, content curation, and tailored user interfaces can significantly enhance user satisfaction and engagement, leading to increased adoption and retention rates. Integrating AI into existing applications can also unlock new revenue streams and business opportunities. By offering AI-powered services or features as premium add-ons or subscriptions, organizations can differentiate their products and create additional sources of recurring revenue.

However, integrating AI into existing applications requires careful planning and a well-defined strategy. Developers must consider factors such as data privacy, security, scalability, and ethical considerations to ensure a seamless and responsible integration process.

Exploring Emerging AI Development Frameworks

The field of AI development is rapidly evolving, with new frameworks and tools emerging constantly to address the growing demand for AI-powered solutions. Keeping up with these advancements is crucial for developers and organizations seeking to stay ahead of the curve and leverage the latest technologies. Emerging AI development frameworks often focus on specific domains or applications, such as natural language processing, computer vision, or predictive analytics. These frameworks provide pre-built models, libraries, and tools that developers can utilize to accelerate the development of AI-powered applications within their respective domains.

Additionally, many of these frameworks are designed to simplify the integration of AI capabilities into existing applications, enabling developers to leverage the power of AI without extensive expertise in machine learning or deep learning algorithms. By exploring and experimenting with emerging AI development frameworks, developers can gain valuable insights into the latest trends and best practices in the field. This knowledge can inform architectural decisions, technology selections, and overall development strategies, ensuring that the solutions they create are future-proof and scalable.

Furthermore, engaging with the vibrant communities surrounding these frameworks can foster collaboration, knowledge-sharing, and cross-pollination of ideas, ultimately driving innovation and pushing the boundaries of what is possible with AI-powered software development.

Upcoming Features and Enhancements

Microsoft is continuously working to improve and expand the capabilities of Copilot AI. Upcoming releases are expected to include enhanced natural language processing, allowing for even more human-like and contextual responses. Additionally, improved multi-modal understanding will enable Copilot to better interpret and generate content across different formats, such as images, videos, and audio. One highly anticipated feature is real-time collaboration, where multiple users can interact with Copilot simultaneously, enabling seamless teamwork and co-creation. Furthermore, personalization options will allow users to fine-tune Copilot's behavior and outputs to better align with their preferences and goals.

Expanding AI Capabilities

As Microsoft's AI research and development teams push the boundaries of what's possible, we can expect to see Copilot's capabilities expand into new domains. For instance, advanced reasoning and problem-solving abilities could empower Copilot to tackle complex analytical tasks, providing valuable insights and recommendations across various industries. Furthermore, the integration of specialized knowledge bases and domain-specific models will enable Copilot to offer expert-level assistance in fields such as healthcare, finance, and legal services. This expansion could revolutionize how professionals access and leverage specialized knowledge, streamlining workflows and driving innovation.

Predictions for AI in Business Tools

The future of AI in business tools is poised to be transformative. As AI technologies like Copilot become more deeply integrated into productivity suites and enterprise software, we can anticipate a significant boost in efficiency and automation across various business processes. For example, AI-powered writing assistants could help professionals craft high-quality documents, reports, and presentations with ease, saving time and ensuring consistent quality. Intelligent scheduling and task management tools could optimize workflows, prioritize tasks, and provide data-driven recommendations for better decision-making.

Moreover, AI-driven analytics and visualization tools could uncover valuable insights from vast datasets, enabling businesses to make informed strategic decisions and gain a competitive edge in their respective markets.

Microsoft's Vision for AI Integration

Microsoft's vision for AI integration extends far beyond individual tools and applications. The company aims to create a seamless and unified AI experience across its entire ecosystem, allowing users to leverage the power of AI seamlessly across different platforms and devices. This vision includes the development of a robust AI infrastructure, enabling Copilot and other AI-powered tools to access and integrate data from various sources, including cloud services, local applications, and IoT devices. This level of integration could revolutionize how we interact with technology, blurring the lines between human and machine capabilities.

In addition, Microsoft is committed to ensuring that its AI technologies are developed and deployed responsibly, with a strong emphasis on ethics, privacy, and security.

This approach aims to foster trust and confidence in AI solutions, enabling broader adoption and fostering a future where AI works alongside humans, augmenting our abilities while respecting our values and rights.

CONCLUSION

In conclusion, it's remarkable to reflect on the transformative power of AI and the boundless opportunities it presents for creating a sustainable online business. By harnessing the capabilities of Microsoft's cutting-edge AI tools, you've gained a competitive edge in the ever-evolving digital landscape.

Throughout this comprehensive guide, we've explored the intricate workings of Microsoft's AI ecosystem, from leveraging the versatility of Office 365 and Azure AI to unlocking the potential of Designer, Teams, and the Power Platform. With each chapter, you've acquired invaluable insights and actionable strategies to capitalize on the remarkable capabilities of these tools. One of the key takeaways is the importance of identifying niche markets and crafting compelling AI solutions tailored to their unique needs. By embracing this approach, you've learned to stand out in a crowded marketplace, captivating your target audience with innovative and impactful offerings.

Furthermore, we've delved into the art of optimizing

documents and presentations, ensuring that your creations resonate with audiences and leave a lasting impression. From crafting compelling narratives to incorporating visually stunning elements, you now possess the skills to elevate your brand and captivate your clientele. Securing funding and developing a robust business plan have also been integral components of our journey. By mastering these critical aspects, you've laid a solid foundation for sustainable growth and long-term success in the ever-changing business landscape.

Moreover, we've explored effective marketing strategies tailored specifically to the unique demands of AI products and services. By leveraging these powerful techniques, you can effectively promote your offerings, reach your target audience, and establish a strong online presence. Undoubtedly, the path ahead is brimming with both challenges and opportunities. However, armed with the knowledge and expertise acquired throughout this guide, you are well-equipped to navigate the complexities of the AI startup ecosystem with confidence and resilience.

Remember, the key to success lies in continuous learning, adaptation, and a relentless pursuit of innovation. Embrace the principles outlined in this guide, and you'll be poised to revolutionize your online business, unlocking new realms of growth and profitability. As you embark on this exhilarating journey, never lose sight of your passion, determination, and unwavering commitment to excellence. The AI world is constantly evolving, and by staying ahead of the curve, you'll not only thrive but also contribute to shaping the future of business and technology.

Congratulations on taking this bold step towards leveraging the power of Microsoft's AI tools to transform your financial future. Opportunities abound ahead, and the knowledge you've gained opens up truly limitless possibilities. Embrace the future, and let your vision soar!

www.ingramcontent.com/pod-product-compliance
Lightning Source LLC
Chambersburg PA
CBHW050014230526
45470CB00003B/955